Age 4+

BIBLE
Coloring Book for Kids

All About Me

My Name is

This is Me!

I am [ ] years old

My Birthday is

_____

My Favorite:

I like to play

Color _____

Animal _____

Prepare yourself to start the fascinating Bible journey!

52 Most well-known stories from the Bible with detailed descriptions and references.

52 Illustrations beautifully drawn wich depict key scenes from each story, making it easy for you to understand and remember the Lessons taught in each one

God creates the world.

Genesis 1:1—2:25

In the beginning, before anything was anything, God made the heavens and the earth. He just said, "Let there be light," and there was light! Then God made the sky and the land and the oceans. God made the plants and the sun, moon, and stars. He liked what He made. It was very good!

Then God said, "Let the sky be filled with birds that fly." And it was. He said, "Let the waters be filled with all sorts of creatures." Then there were fish, dolphins, jellyfish, and many other creatures in the water. Next, God made every kind of animal. When God saw all the creatures that He made, He said that they were very good.

Then God did something even more special! He took some dirt and formed it into a man. Then God breathed into the man and he became alive. Next, God made a woman. They were the first people—people like you and me. They were named Adam and Eve. God loved Adam and Eve. Everything God made was very good.

God creates the world.

Genesis 1:1—2:25

Adam and Eve disobey God.

Genesis 3:1-24

Adam and Eve lived in a wonderful garden. There were trees and plants with good food like apples, bananas, grapes, and watermelon. There were flowers and trees and plants that were beautiful to look at.

In the middle of the garden was a tree called the Tree of the Knowledge of good and evil. God told Adam and Eve they could eat anything in the whole garden except the fruit that was growing on that one tree.

One day, a serpent talked to Eve and told her to eat the forbidden fruit. "If you eat some of that fruit, you would know things you didn't know before," the snake said. "You would be like God."

Eve listened to the serpent. She ate some of the fruit from the tree that God said not to eat from. Adam ate some, too. God was very sad that they had disobeyed Him. Adam and Eve had to leave the beautiful garden, but God still loved them very much.

Adam and Eve disobey God.
Genesis 3:1-24

Noah builds an ark.

Genesis 6:1-22

Adam and Eve had children, and their children had children. After a while, there were many people everywhere. But they did not love and obey God. They hurt other people and did not follow God's rules. God was sorry He had made them.

There was one person left who loved God. His name was Noah. Noah did what was right. God told Noah that He was going to send a flood to cover the whole world.

"Make a big boat," God told Noah. The boat was called an ark. Noah and his family would be safe in the ark when the flood came.

Noah and his family obeyed God. They worked hard to build the ark. They worked hard to gather lots of food. After a long time, the ark was ready. Noah and his family were ready.

Noah builds an ark.

Genesis 6:1-22

God makes a promise.

Genesis 8:1—9:17

The earth was covered with water for a long time. Finally, the water went away enough for the bottom of the ark to rest on a mountain. The earth began to dry up.

Noah and his family and all the animals stayed on the ark for many days. When the earth was dry enough, God told Noah to come out of the ark. Noah's family must have been so excited! The animals must have been very excited, too. It had been a long time since they had been able to run and climb and leap on dry ground.

After he let all the animals out of the ark, Noah built an altar, a special place to worship God. Noah thanked God for keeping his family safe during the flood.

God was happy to hear Noah praying. He promised Noah that He would never again destroy all living things with a flood. God put a rainbow in the sky to remind everyone of His promise.

God makes a promise.
Genesis 8:1—9:17

Abram travels to a new home.

Genesis 12:1-9

God loved Abram. God told Abram to leave his home and go to a new land. God promised to make Abram the leader of a great nation.

Abram obeyed God. He and his wife and his nephew, Lot, left their home. They took all their animals and their helpers with them. They walked for many, many days.

After days and days of walking, Abram and his family arrived in the new land. God told him that He was going to give the land to Abram's children. Abram worshiped God. Abram trusted God. Abram believed that God would keep His promises.

Abram travels to a new home.
Genesis 12:1-9

Isaac is born.

Genesis 15:1-6; 17:1-8; 18:1-15; 21:1-7

God gave a special promise to Abram. He promised to give Abram and his wife have a son. As a reminder of His promise, God changed Abram's name to Abraham. Abraham means "father of many." Abraham and his wife, Sarah, waited many years but they still did not have a child. Abraham still did not stop believing God's promise.

Abraham and Sarah grew very old, older than most grandparents. One day some angels visited Abraham. "Next year Sarah will have a son," the visitors said.
Sarah was sitting in her tent listening to Abraham and the visitors. When she heard the angel's words, she started to laugh. She and Abraham were almost one hundred years old!

She knew that no one her age ever had a baby. She was just too old! The visitors knew that she laughed. They said, "Is anything too hard for God?"
God kept His promise to Abraham and Sarah. The next year, Sarah had a baby boy just as God had said. Abraham and Sarah named him Isaac.

Isaac is born.

Genesis 15:1-6; 17:1-8; 18:1-15; 21:1-7

Abraham's servant finds a wife for Isaac.

Genesis 24:1-67

Isaac grew up and soon it was time for him to get married. Abraham talked to his servant. "Promise me that you will find a wife for my son Isaac." His servant promised to do his best.

The servant loaded many gifts on some camels. He traveled through the hot, dry desert to the land where Abraham used to live. Abraham's servant stopped by the well in a town. The servant asked God to show him who Isaac's new wife would be.

While he was praying, a beautiful woman named Rebekah came to the well. Abraham's servant asked her for some water. She gave him a drink and then said, "I'll give water to your camels, also." Rebekah worked hard pouring water into the watering trough until the thirsty camels had enough water. Abraham's servant knew that this kind of person was the one God wanted to be Isaac's wife.

Abraham's servant was glad that God answered his prayer. Rebekah was happy to be Isaac's wife.

Abraham's servant finds a wife for Isaac.
Genesis 24:1-67

Jacob tricks Esau.
Genesis 25:19-34; 27:1-41

Jacob and Esau were twin brothers. Esau was born first, so he was supposed to be the next leader of the family. Esau loved to hunt and be outside. Jacob was quiet and stayed at home.

One day Jacob was cooking some stew. Esau came home from hunting and he was very hungry. "Give me some of your stew," he said.

"I'll give you some stew if you give me the right to lead the family when our father dies," Jacob answered. So Esau gave his birthright to Jacob. Esau wanted the stew more than he wanted to be his family's leader.

Another time, Jacob dressed up like Esau. Jacob put some goat's skin on his arms and chest so he would feel hairy like Esau. Jacob put on some of Esau's clothes so he would smell sweaty like Esau. (They didn't wash their clothes very often back then!)

Jacob talked to Isaac, but because Isaac was almost blind Isaac thought Jacob was really Esau! Isaac prayed for Jacob, and made promises to him, promises he had meant to make to Esau. When Esau found out about Jacob's trick he was very angry.

Jacob tricks Esau.

Genesis 25:19-34; 27:1-41

Joseph forgives his brothers.

Genesis 42:1—45:28

Jacob's family didn't have any food. Jacob heard that there was food to buy in Egypt. He sent Joseph's brothers there to buy food. Joseph's brothers didn't know that God had helped Joseph become an important ruler in Egypt.

When Joseph's brothers got to Egypt, they asked to buy food. They did not know they were talking to Joseph. It had been a long time since they had seen Joseph. Joseph had grown up. Now he dressed and talked like an Egyptian.

Joseph pretended that he did not know his brothers. He asked them about their family. Joseph tested them to see if they were sorry for being mean to him. Then Joseph told his brothers who he was, and he forgave them. Joseph invited them all to come and live near him in Egypt. Joseph was glad to be with his family again.

Joseph forgives his brothers.

Genesis 42:1—45:28

The people of Israel are slaves in Egypt.

Exodus 1:1-22

Joseph's brothers and father and all their families moved to Egypt. They lived there for many years. They had children and their children had children. They were called Israelites. Soon there were many Israelites in Egypt.

There was a new king in Egypt now. This Pharaoh didn't know the good things that Joseph had done for his country. He was afraid of the Israelites because there were so many of them. He thought they might take over the country. The new Pharaoh made the Israelites his slaves. That means he made them work hard and didn't pay them.

Even though the Egyptians treated the Israelite slaves very badly, God had the plan to help the Israelites.

The people of Israel are slaves in Egypt.
Exodus 1:1-22

God protects baby Moses.

Exodus 2:1-10

Pharaoh was afraid of the Israelites. There were many Israelites in Egypt. Pharaoh thought there were too many Israelites. Pharaoh planned to stop them by hurting all the Israelite baby boys.

But one mother hid her baby boy from the Egyptian soldiers.

When she couldn't hide him anymore, she made a basket that would float. She put the baby in the basket and carefully put it in the river. The baby's big sister, Miriam, hid nearby to watch what would happen.

Pharaoh's daughter came to the river with her servants to take a bath. The princess saw the basket and sent one of her servants to get it. When she opened the basket, the baby was crying. The Princess felt sorry for him.

Miriam ran up to the princess and said, "Shall I go and get someone to take care of this baby for you?" The princess said yes. So Miriam brought her mother to the princess. The princess told the mother to take care of the baby. Later the princess named the baby Moses. When Moses grew up, he lived with the princess, right in the Pharaoh's palace!

God protects baby Moses.
Exodus 2:1-10

God talks to Moses.

Exodus 3:1—4:17

Grown-up Moses went to live in the desert. He took care of some sheep. One day he saw something strange. A bush was on fire, but it did not burn up! Moses walked near the bush to see why it didn't burn up.

God spoke to Moses from the bush. He said, "Moses, take off your shoes. This is a holy place." Moses knew it was God talking. God said, "Moses, tell Pharaoh to let my people go free." God did not want the Israelites to be slaves anymore. God wanted Moses to be the leader of the Israelites.

Moses was afraid. He was afraid that Pharaoh would not listen to him. Moses was afraid that the Israelites would not listen to him.

God told Moses that He would help Moses do what God wanted.

Moses would even be able to do miracles. Then Pharaoh would do what God wanted. But Moses was still afraid. So God told Moses that Moses' brother Aaron would help him. Finally, Moses was ready to go talk to Pharaoh.

God talks to Moses.

Exodus 3:1—4:17

God makes a path through the Red Sea.

Exodus 14:1-31

Pharaoh wanted the Israelites to come back to Egypt. He didn't have enough slaves left to do all the work the Israelites had done before they left.

So Pharaoh and his army chased after the Israelites. When the people saw the army coming, they were afraid. They couldn't run away because they were at the edge of the Red Sea. But God took care of His people. God told Moses to hold his hand out over the Red Sea.
God sent a strong wind that blew and blew and made a path of dry land through the Red Sea. The people walked through the sea on dry ground!

The Egyptian army tried to follow them. When all the Israelites were safe on the other side, God told Moses to stretch his hand out over the sea again. The water went back into its place. Whoosh! The Egyptian army was covered up by the water.
All the Israelites trusted God because of the way He saved them from the Egyptians.

God makes a path through the Red Sea.
Exodus 14:1-31

God gives the Ten Commandments.

Exodus 19:1—24:18

The Israelites walked in the desert for many days. They came to a mountain. God told them to camp by the mountain. All the people set up tents. They gathered fuel and made fires to cook food on. They found places for their animals to rest and eat.

God told Moses to come up to the top of the mountain.
God wanted to talk with Moses. God told Moses many things while Moses was on the mountain.
God gave Moses two stone tablets on that God wrote His laws on. God told Moses many more laws for the people to follow. God's laws helped the people know what God wanted. God's laws told the people to be fair to each other.

Moses went down from the mountain and told the Israelites everything God had told him. The people promised to obey God.

God gives the Ten Commandments.

Exodus 19:1—24:18

God provides water from a rock.

Numbers 20:1-13

The people were thirsty. They came to Moses. "Why did you make us come out here to the desert?" they said. "Why did you make us leave Egypt? There is nothing good to eat here. There is no water."

Moses was angry with the people. They blamed him for all their problems. They forgot how God protected them and always cared for them. So Moses talked to God.

God told Moses to speak to a rock in front of the people. God would make water come out of the rock. Moses went to the rock. But Moses was so angry, he didn't do what God said. Instead of speaking to the rock, Moses hit the rock with his staff! God made water come out of the rock even though Moses didn't do what God said. God was sad that Moses didn't obey Him.

God provides water from a rock.

Numbers 20:1-13

Rahab helps two spies.
Joshua 2:1-24

Joshua was the new leader of God's people. God told Joshua to lead the people into the Promised Land. God promised to be with Joshua. "Be strong and courageous," God said.

Joshua sent two spies to Jericho to look at the land. The king of Jericho heard about the spies and sent soldiers to find them. The spies were in the house of a woman named Rahab. She hid them on the roof of her house under some stalks of flax. When the soldiers came to her house, she told the soldiers that the men had already left the city.

The soldiers hurried out of the city to find the spies. Then Rahab helped the spies escape. Her house was on the wall of the city. The spies climbed down over the wall using a rope. Rahab asked the spies to keep her safe when they took over the land. The spies promised that no one in her house would be hurt if she left the rope hanging in the window.

Rahab helps two spies.
Joshua 2:1-24

The walls of Jericho fall down.

Joshua 6:1-27

Joshua and the Israelites were camped outside Jericho. The people of Jericho closed the gates to the city and didn't let anyone in or out. They were afraid. They didn't want the Israelites to take over their city.

God told Joshua a plan to take over the city. Joshua and the Israelites did just what God said. Very quietly, they stood in a line. They didn't say a word. They marched all the way around Jericho. They did this every day for almost a whole week.

On the last day, they marched around the city one, two, three, four, five, six, and seven times. Then they stopped. The priests blew the trumpets and all the people shouted. Then the walls fell down flat! The Israelites marched straight into the city.

The walls of Jericho fall down.
Joshua 6:1-27

Ruth shows love.
Ruth 1:1-22

Naomi and her family lived in Israel. But there wasn't much food in Israel anymore. So Naomi and her family went to live in Moab. There was plenty of food in Moab.

Naomi's two sons grew up and got married. One of them married Ruth. After a while, Naomi's sons and husband died. Naomi was sad. She heard that there was food in Israel again, so she decided to go home.

Ruth wanted to go with Naomi. "Stay here in Moab," Naomi said. "I don't have any money. You would be poor if you stayed with me."

"Please don't tell me to leave you," Ruth said. "I will go wherever you go. Your people will be my people and your God my God." Ruth stayed with Naomi because she loved Naomi and she loved God. Ruth didn't mind that they were very poor and didn't have any way to make money.

Ruth shows love.
Ruth 1:1-22

God helps Gideon defeat the Midianites.

Judges 7:1-21

Many people came to help Gideon fight the Midianites. But many of the men were afraid. "Let everyone who is afraid go home," God told Gideon. Most of the men left.

But God thought Gideon's army was still too big. God told Gideon takes the men to the river to get a drink. Most of the men got down on their knees to drink. God told Gideon to send those men home.

Now only three hundred men were left. That was not very many! The army from Midian had more men than Gideon could count. There was no way that only three hundred men could win a battle against such a big army!

God told Gideon what to do. Gideon gave each man in his army a trumpet and a jar with a torch inside. The men surrounded the Midianite camp.

At just the right time they blew their trumpets, broke their jars , and shouted, "The sword of the Lord and Gideon!" When the big Midianite army heard the noise and saw the lights, they ran away! God saved His people with a small army and a leader who obeyed God.

God helps Gideon defeat the Midianites.

Judges 7:1-21

God answers Hannah's prayer.

1 Samuel 1:1—2:11

Hannah's husband had another wife named Peninnah. Peninnah had sons and daughters, but Hannah didn't have any children. Peninnah made fun of Hannah because she didn't have children. Hannah felt sad.

When Hannah's family went to worship God at the Tabernacle, Hannah cried and cried. She prayed, "Please God, give me a son."

Eli, the priest, saw Hannah praying and thought she was drunk. He told Hannah to stop getting drunk. Hannah said, "I am not drunk. I am very sad and am asking God to help me." Eli told her to go in peace. Eli asked God to give her what she asked for. God answered Hannah's prayer. Hannah named her baby boy Samuel. When he was old enough, Hannah took Samuel to the Tabernacle so that he could serve God.

God answers Hannah's prayer.

1 Samuel 1:1—2:11

Samuel chooses a king.

1 Samuel 8:1—10:24

Samuel grew up to be the leader of Israel. He was called a judge. Now Samuel was getting old. Some people talked to Samuel. They said, "Give us a king like all the other countries around us. We want to be like them."

Samuel was upset because he knew God was the real King of Israel! So he prayed to God. God said, "Samuel, warn them. Tell them that a king will make them his servants and will take their land and animals."

Samuel told the people all the things God had said. The people didn't care! They said, "We want a king anyway!"

About that time, a young man named Saul was out looking for his father's lost donkeys. As Saul walked into town, Samuel saw Saul. God said, "Samuel, here's the man I want to be king."

Samuel said to Saul, "I'd like you to come and eat with me. And don't worry, your donkeys have been found." The next morning, Samuel took a small bottle of olive oil and poured it on Saul's head saying, "The Lord has chosen you to be the leader of His people." And from that time, God helped Saul become ready to be king.

Samuel chooses a king.

1 Samuel 8:1—10:24

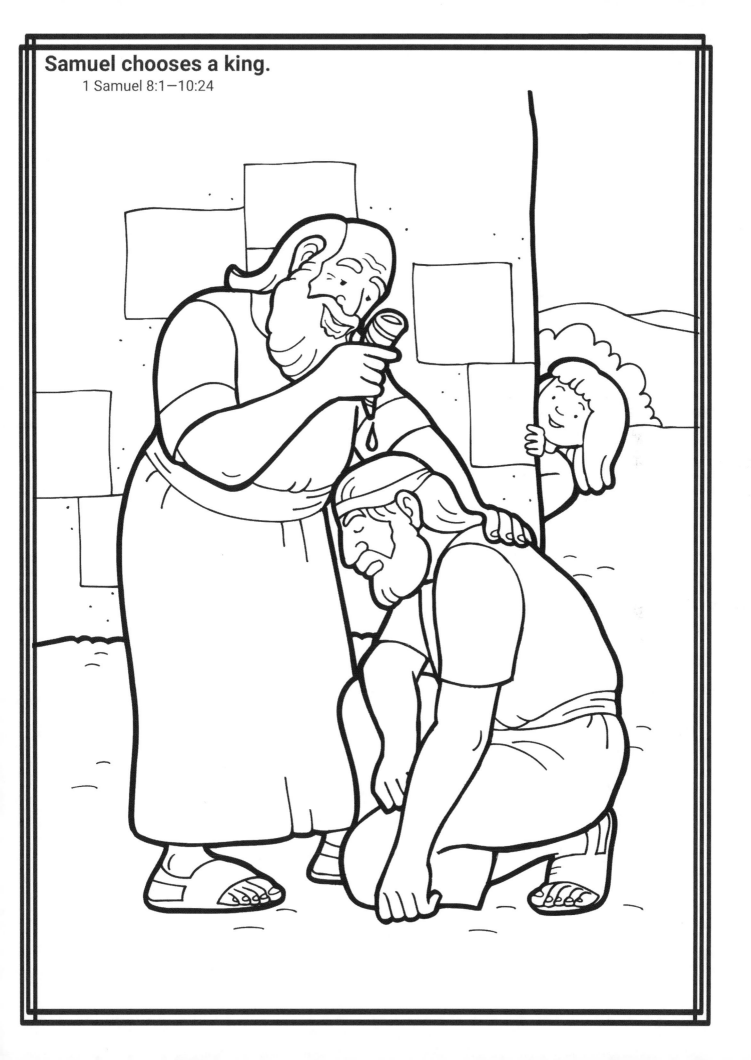

David fights Goliath.
1 Samuel 17:1-58

David's brothers were in Saul's army. One day, David's father sent him to visit his brothers. David saw the army getting ready to fight the Philistines. Suddenly, a giant Philistine came out. Saul's army was afraid. They ran back to their tents.

Goliath, the Philistine giant, was more than nine feet tall. Goliath yelled, "Choose a man to fight me. If he is able to kill me, we will become your slaves. But if I win the fight, you will become our slaves." No one in the Israelite camp wanted to fight Goliath. They didn't think anyone could beat someone so big!

David knew that God was stronger than Goliath. David said, "I'll go and fight him." King Saul heard what David said. "You're too young and small to fight Goliath," King Saul said.
"But God helped me fight lions and bears when I took care of my father's sheep, and God will help me now," David answered.
Goliath laughed when he saw David. He even made fun of God!
David used just his slingshot and a stone to fight Goliath. God helped David save his people from the Philistine army.

David fights Goliath.
1 Samuel 17:1-58

God sends ravens with food for Elijah.

1 Kings 17:1-6

Ahab was the new king of Israel. Ahab didn't worship God. Ahab built places to worship idols instead of God. Many of the people in Israel stopped worshiping God because of the evil things that Ahab did. God was angry with Ahab.

Elijah didn't worship idols. Elijah obeyed God. Elijah went to see King Ahab. "There won't be any rain for a long time," Elijah said. "There won't be any rain to make the food in the fields grow. There won't be any rain to make the grass green. There won't be any rain to give the people water to drink." Ahab was very angry. So God told Elijah to hide from the king. Elijah left the city. He walked and walked. Elijah came to a brook. Elijah drank some water from the brook. God told Elijah to stay by the brook. God told Elijah that birds called ravens were going to bring food to him.

Every morning and every evening the ravens came with bread and meat for Elijah to eat.

God sends ravens with food for Elijah.
1 Kings 17:1-6

Elijah goes to heaven.

2 Kings 2:1-14

Elijah was an important prophet who told people messages from God. But it was time for Elijah to leave and go to heaven. Elijah and Elisha walked together. They crossed a river. Elijah said, "If God lets you see me when I go up to heaven, then you will take over my job."

Suddenly a chariot and some horses that looked like fire swooped down out of the sky! Then Elijah went to heaven in a whirlwind. All that was left was Elijah's cloak which had fallen to the ground. Elisha picked up the cloak.

Elisha had seen the chariot and the horses. It was very exciting! Elisha was sad that Elijah was not going to be with him anymore, but now Elisha had an important job to do. Elisha knew God was with him and would help him.

Josiah hears God's Word.

2 Kings 22:1—23:3; 2 Chronicles 34:14-32

Josiah was only eight years old when he became king. No one in his country read God's Word anymore. Even the priests who were in charge of the Temple didn't know where God's Word was!

One day a priest in the Temple found a scroll with God's Word written on it. He ran to the king's helper. "Here is a scroll with God's Word written on it!" the priest said. "King Josiah will want to see this!" The helper took the scroll to the king.

The king's helper read God's Word to Josiah. King Josiah listened to God's Word. King Josiah loved God and wanted to obey God's Word, but when he heard what was written in God's Word, he cried. It made him sad to learn that his people were not obeying God.

King Josiah called all the leaders together. He told them what God's Word said. Josiah and all the leaders promised to obey God's Word.

Josiah hears God's Word.

2 Kings 22:1—23:3; 2 Chronicles 34:14-32

Jonah disobeys God.
Jonah 1:1—2:10

God was not happy with the way the people in Nineveh acted. God told Jonah to warn the people in Nineveh that God would punish them for all the bad things they kept doing. But Jonah didn't like the people in Nineveh and didn't want them to get a warning. So Jonah decided to disobey God. Jonah got on a boat that was going the other way.

God wanted Jonah to obey Him. God sent a storm that made the boat start to sink. The people on the boat were afraid. Jonah said, "God sent this storm because I ran away from Him. If you want this storm to stop, you must throw me overboard." The people on the boat threw Jonah into the water. Suddenly, the sea was still.

Jonah went down, down, down. Jonah wanted to breathe, but he couldn't. Jonah saw a giant fish swimming toward him! Jonah tried to swim away, but the giant fish opened its giant mouth and swallowed Jonah. Gulp!

Jonah was in the belly of the big fish. Now Jonah could breathe. It must have been very smelly! Jonah was sorry he had disobeyed God. He prayed and promised to obey God. Finally, God made the fish swim to the shore and spit Jonah up on the beach.

Jonah disobeys God.
Jonah 1:1—2:10

Daniel and his friends choose to obey God.

Daniel 1:1-21

Daniel and his friends were taken to a faraway palace. The king wanted them to learn to work for him. The king gave them some special food. Daniel and his friends knew that God did not want them to eat the kind of food that the king gave them.

Daniel and his friends wanted to obey God. Daniel asked the king's helper to give his friends only vegetables and water. The king's helper was afraid that Daniel and his friends would not be as healthy as some of the other boys who were learning to work for the king. The king's helper knew that the king would be angry if Daniel and his friends were not healthy.

Daniel said, "Please test us for ten days. Give us only vegetables and water and then see who is healthiest—my friends and I or the others." The king's helper agreed to test them.

After ten days, Daniel and his friends looked healthier than any of the other young men. God helped Daniel and his friends. The king liked Daniel and his friends. He gave them important jobs.

Daniel and his friends choose to obey God.

Daniel 1:1-21

God protects Daniel's friends in a furnace.

Daniel 3:1-30

King Nebuchadnezzar built a tall, tall statue. King Nebuchadnezzar wanted everyone to bow down and worship his statue. The king said, "Anyone who does not bow down will be thrown into a blazing furnace!"

Some men who worked for the king saw that Shadrach, Meshach, and Abednego did not bow down to the king's statue. They did not bow down because they knew they should only worship God, not a statue.

The king was very angry with the three men. The king ordered his guards to tie up Shadrach, Meshach, and Abednego and throw them into the hottest furnace. But when they were in the furnace, the king saw something very strange. Shadrach, Meshach, and Abednego were not being burned up! They were not even tied up anymore. They were walking around inside the furnace with another person—an angel!

The king called to Shadrach, Meshach, and Abednego, "Servants of the Highest God, come out!" The king said, "Praise God who sent an angel to save His servants. Shadrach, Meshach, and Abednego would rather give up their lives than worship any god other than the one true God."

God protects Daniel's friends in a furnace.

Daniel 3:1-30

God protects Daniel in a den of lions.

Daniel 6:1-28

Daniel loved God and prayed to Him every day. In fact, he prayed three times every day. Daniel knew that praying to God was the right thing to do.

There were some mean men who did not like Daniel. They went to the king and said, "King, we think you should make a rule that everyone must pray only to you. If people pray to anyone else but you, they will be thrown into a cave filled with lions!" The king thought this was a good idea.

The next day Daniel prayed to God. The mean men watched as Daniel prayed to God. Then they ran to tell the king what they saw. The king was sad. Daniel was his friend. The king knew he had been tricked into hurting Daniel.

 But the king had to obey the rule, too. Daniel was put into a big cave where hungry lions lived.

All night the king worried about Daniel. The next morning, the king ran to the lions' cave. He called, "Daniel! Daniel!" Daniel called out, "King, I am safe. The Lord God took care of me!"

The king was so glad that Daniel was not hurt. Then the king told everyone what God had done.

God protects Daniel in a den of lions.
Daniel 6:1-28

Esther is chosen queen.

Esther 2:1-18

The queen didn't do what King Xerxes wanted. The king was very angry. "What should I do?" the king asked his friends. The king's friends said, "Send her away and find a new queen." So the king started looking for a new queen. Many beautiful girls in the kingdom were brought to the palace.

One girl who was brought to the palace was named Esther. Esther was very beautiful. Esther met the king. The king liked Esther. The king said, "I want Esther to be the new queen." The king put a crown on Esther's head. The king invited many people to a banquet for Queen Esther. The king was so happy that he told everyone to take a holiday. The king didn't know that God had a special job for Esther to do.

Esther is chosen queen.
Esther 2:1-18

Nehemiah rebuilds the walls.

Nehemiah 2:11—4:23

Nehemiah was the king's special helper. One day, Nehemiah's brother came from far away to visit him. "The city where we used to live had strong walls. Now they are broken. The city is not safe."

Nehemiah was sad. So Nehemiah prayed to God.

When the king saw Nehemiah he asked him, "Why are you so sad?" Nehemiah said, "I am sad because the wall around my city is broken down."

The king said, "You may go and help the people build the wall. Come back when it is finished." Nehemiah was very happy.

When Nehemiah came to the city, he said to all the people, "We can build the wall. We can make it strong again."

Everyone worked together. After many days, the wall was finished. Everyone was glad to see the wall. And Nehemiah was glad God had heard his prayer.

Nehemiah rebuilds the walls.
Nehemiah 2:11—4:23

An angel visits Mary.

Luke 1:26-38

God wanted to tell a girl named Mary some good news. When you tell someone good news, you might call on the telephone or write a letter. But God sent an angel to talk to Mary!

One day Mary was alone. She looked up. Standing right there beside her was an angel! Mary had never seen a real angel before. Mary was surprised to see the angel. She was afraid. The angel said, "Don't be afraid, Mary. God loves you. He has chosen you to be the mother of a very special baby. You will name the baby Jesus. This special baby will be God's own Son!"

Mary was glad to hear this promise. She praised God.

An angel visits Mary.
Luke 1:26-38

Jesus is born.
Luke 2:1-7

Mary was going to have a baby. An angel had come to tell Mary about this baby. Her baby would be special. He would be God's Son. When it was time to have her baby, Mary and Joseph had to take a trip. They walked and walked for three days. Finally, Mary and Joseph came to Bethlehem. There were so many people that there weren't any rooms left in the inn. There wasn't anywhere else for them to stay.

Finally, Mary and Joseph found a place to stay. It wasn't a nice place. It probably wasn't even a clean place. It was a place for animals to stay! Mary's little baby was born there. Mary wrapped the little baby in some clean cloths and then she laid Him in a manger filled with clean straws. Mary and Joseph named this baby Jesus.

Jesus is born.
Luke 2:1-7

Mary and Joseph look for Jesus.

Luke 2:41-52

Crowds of people were on their way home. They had been to Jerusalem for a special celebration. Mary and Joseph were there. They were walking and talking with their friends. They thought Jesus was there in the crowd, too. They thought Jesus was walking and talking with His friends.

Mary and Joseph and their friends walked all day. When it began to get dark, Mary and Joseph started looking for Jesus. *Jesus should be here somewhere*Mary must have thought. Mary and Joseph did not find Jesus. Mary and Joseph were worried. *What happened to Jesus? Did He get hurt? Is He lost?*

They hurried back to Jerusalem. Mary and Joseph looked and looked. Finally, they found Jesus. He was sitting in the Temple! Jesus was listening to the teachers. Jesus was asking them questions. The teachers were amazed at Jesus. The teachers were learning from Jesus even though He was just a boy. Mary asked Jesus, "Why are you here? We have been looking for you." Jesus said, "Why were you looking for me? Didn't you know I had to be in my Father's house?" Jesus went home with Mary and Joseph. Jesus obeyed them.

Mary and Joseph look for Jesus.
Luke 2:41-52

John baptizes Jesus.

Matthew 3:13-17; Mark 1:9-11; Luke 3:21,22; John 1:29-34

One day Jesus went to see John the Baptist. John was preaching and baptizing people in the Jordan River. John told people to turn away from doing bad things because the Savior of the world was coming.

Jesus asked John to baptize Him. John knew that Jesus was the Savior of the world. John said, "I am not even good enough to tie your shoes. Why do you ask me to baptize you? You ought to baptize me!" Jesus said that it was right for John to baptize Him.

So John and Jesus waded out into the river. After John baptized Jesus, a dove flew down and landed on Jesus to show that God was with Him. A voice from heaven said, "This is my Son. I am pleased with Him."

John baptizes Jesus.

Matthew 3:13-17; Mark 1:9-11;
Luke 3:21,22; John 1:29-34

Jesus says, "Follow me."

Matthew 4:18-22; Mark 1:16-20; Luke 5:1-11; John 1:40-42

Peter and Andrew liked to fish. They went fishing every day. Fishing was how they earned money.

One day Jesus came to the Sea of Galilee where they were fishing. Many people wanted to hear Jesus teach. The people kept crowding around Him, trying to get closer. Jesus got into Peter and Andrew's boat. Then Jesus sat down and taught all the people who were crowded on the beach.

When Jesus finished talking to the people, Jesus told Peter to take the boat out into deeper water. Then Jesus told Peter to let down his nets to catch some fish.

When Peter and Andrew let down the nets, they caught so many fish that the nets began to break! Peter and Andrew called their partners in another boat to come and help them. There were so many fish that when they pulled the nets with the fish into the boats, the boats began to sink. Quickly, the men rowed to shore. Jesus said, "From now on you will catch people." Jesus meant Peter and Andrew would tell lots of people the good news about Jesus. Peter and Andrew and their partners pulled their boats up on the beach, left everything, and followed Jesus.

Jesus says, "Follow me."
Matthew 4:18-22; Mark 1:16-20; Luke 5:1-11; John 1:40-42

Jesus talks to a Samaritan woman.

John 4:1-42

Jesus and His friends walked to the country of Samaria. It was a long walk. Jesus was tired, so He sat down by a well to rest. Jesus' friends went into town to find some food to eat.

While Jesus' friends were gone, a woman came to the well to get some water. It was very hot outside. The sun was very bright. The woman brought a big jar to fill with water. It must have been hard work to carry the heavy jar.

"May I have a drink?" Jesus asked. The woman was surprised! Men never talked to women in public places back then. Jesus told the woman some secrets she had. Jesus showed her that He cared about her. Jesus told her He was the Messiah—the Savior God promised to send. The woman went back to the town to tell others about Jesus. She brought many people back to see Jesus so they could hear Him, too.

Jesus talks to a Samaritan woman.

John 4:1-42

Jesus heals Jairus's daughter.

Matthew 9:18-26; Mark 5:22-43; Luke 8:40-56

Jairus's daughter was sick. Jairus went to see Jesus. "Please come and heal my daughter." Jesus went with Jairus. As they walked to Jairus's house, a helper came and said that Jairus's little girl was already dead.

Jesus said, "Don't be afraid. She will be fine." When they got to Jairus's house, Jesus told everyone to leave the little girl's room. Then Jesus and the little girl's parents went into the room. Jesus took the little girl by the hand and said, "My child, get up!" Right away she stood up. Jesus told her parents to give her something to eat. Her parents were amazed to see Jesus' power over death.

Jesus heals Jairus's daughter.
Matthew 9:18-26; Mark 5:22-43; Luke 8:40-56

Jesus uses a boy's lunch to feed 5,000 people.

Matthew 14:13-21; Mark 6:30-44; Luke 9:10-17; John 6:1-15

Many people followed Jesus. They listened to Him talk all-day long. They didn't have any food to eat and it was getting late. The people were hungry. They were a long way from a town with food. Jesus told His friends to give the people something to eat. Jesus' friends didn't have enough food for all the people. Only one little boy had some food. It was just enough for one person to have lunch, but the little boy wanted to share his food.

Jesus told the people to sit down. Jesus took the boy's lunch and prayed. Then Jesus broke off pieces of bread and fish. His friends gave the food to the people. There was more than enough for everyone to eat. It was a miracle—something only God could do. One little boy's lunch became enough food for everyone to eat!

Jesus uses a boy's lunch to feed 5,000 people.

Matthew 14:13-21; Mark 6:30-44; Luke 9:10-17; John 6:1-15

Jesus loves the children.

Matthew 19:13-15; Mark 10:13-16; Luke 18:15-17

One day Jesus was teaching His friends and other people about God. They were listening carefully to what Jesus was saying. Just then, a group of people came to see Jesus.

Jesus and His friends looked at these people and saw that it was children and their parents. The children and their mothers and fathers were so excited to see Jesus.

But when they came near to Jesus, His friends thought that Jesus was too busy to talk to the children. Jesus' friends said, "Don't bring those children here!" The children and their parents were sad to hear those words. They started to walk away.

But wait! Jesus said, "Let the children come to Me! I want to see them!" Jesus was not too busy to see the children! Jesus loved them!

Right away, the children ran to Jesus. They crowded close to Him. Some even climbed up on His lap. Jesus put His arms around them.

What a happy day! The children knew Jesus loved them!

Jesus loves the children.
Matthew 19:13-15; Mark 10:13-16; Luke 18:15-17

People welcome Jesus to Jerusalem.

Matthew 21:1-11; Mark 11:1-11; Luke 19:28-44

What a happy day! Jesus and His friends were going to the Temple in Jerusalem. On the way, Jesus stopped. He said to His friends, "There is a little donkey in the town. Untie it and bring it to Me."

Jesus climbed onto the donkey's back and began riding to the city. Many other people were walking along the road to Jerusalem. Some people were so happy to see Jesus that they spread their coats on the road. Other people cut branches from palm trees and laid them on the road for Jesus' donkey to walk on. They were treating Jesus like a king!

Some people ran ahead to tell others, "Jesus is coming!" And even more, people came to see Jesus. They said, "Hosanna! Hosanna!" (That means "Save us.") It was a wonderful day in Jerusalem! The people praised Jesus!

People welcome Jesus to Jerusalem.

Matthew 21:1-11; Mark 11:1-11; Luke 19:28-44

Jesus eats a special meal with His friends.

Matthew 26:17-30; Mark 14:12-26; Luke 22:7-38

Jesus and His friends were in Jerusalem to celebrate a holiday together. The holiday was called the Passover. Jewish people celebrate the Passover every year to remind them of the time God freed them from slavery.

As part of the holiday, Jesus and His friends ate a special meal. Jesus picked up some bread from the table. Jesus said thank you to God for the bread. Then Jesus broke the bread into pieces and gave some bread to each of His friends.
"Take and eat. This is my body given for you," Jesus said. He compared the bread to His body.

Then Jesus took a cup and thanked God for it. "Drink from this cup. This is my blood shed for many people," Jesus said. Jesus gave the cup to each friend.

The bread and the cup were reminders of what was going to happen soon: Jesus' death on the cross. This special meal called the Last Supper reminds everyone who follows Jesus of His love and God's plan to forgive sins.

Jesus eats a special meal with His friends.

Matthew 26:17-30; Mark 14:12-26; Luke 22:7-38

Jesus dies on the cross.

Matthew 27:32-56; Mark 15:21-41; Luke 23:26-49; John 19:17-37

One day, Jesus told His friends, "In a few days, some people are going to take Me away. I'm going to be killed." Jesus' friends were sad. Jesus knew this was part of God's plan so people could be forgiven for wrong things they have done. And Jesus knew He wouldn't stay dead!

The people who wanted to kill Jesus did not like that so many people loved Him. When these people came to get Jesus, Jesus let them take Him. And He let them kill Him on the cross. Jesus' friends were sad. They took Jesus' body and put it into a tomb.

A tomb was a little room cut out of the side of a hill. Some men put a huge rock in front of the doorway of the tomb. Jesus' friends were very sad. They didn't know that something wonderful was going to happen.

Jesus dies on the cross.

Matthew 27:32-56; Mark 15:21-41;
Luke 23:26-49; John 19:17-37

Jesus talks to Mary in the garden.

John 20:10-18

Mary felt very sad. She thought she would never see Jesus again. Mary went to the tomb where Jesus' body was. Mary wanted to put some spices on Jesus' body (as people did in Bible times when someone died).

When Mary got to the tomb, she saw that it was empty! Jesus' the body wasn't there anymore. Mary cried and cried. She didn't know that Jesus was alive. Mary saw two angels. They asked, "Why are you crying?"

Mary said, "Someone has taken Jesus' body and I don't know where they have put it." Then Mary turned around and saw a man standing there.

"Woman," the man said, "why are you crying? Whom are you looking for?" Mary thought that He was a gardener.

Mary said, "Sir if you have taken him away, tell me where you have put him."

The man just said her name, "Mary." Right away Mary knew that He was Jesus and He was alive! Mary felt so happy! Jesus told Mary to go and tell His friends that He was alive.

Jesus talks to Mary in the garden.
John 20:10-18

Jesus cooks breakfast on the beach.

John 21:1-25

After Jesus died and came back to life, some of Jesus' friends went fishing. They fished all night long but didn't catch any fish. They were still in their boats on the lake when morning came. As it got light, they could see someone standing on the beach. He called out, "Do you have any fish?"Jesus' friends answered, "No."

"Throw your net on the right side of the boat and you will find some fish," the man said. When Jesus' friends threw out the net, they caught so many fish that they couldn't pull the net back onto the boat. Peter knew it was Jesus talking to them! Peter jumped into the water and swam to the beach to see Jesus. The others followed in the boat. They towed the net full of fish behind them.

When they got to the shore, they saw that Jesus was cooking breakfast. There was a fire with some fish on it and some bread. Jesus invited them to have breakfast with Him.

Jesus cooks breakfast on the beach.
John 21:1-25

Jesus goes back to heaven.

Luke 24:50-53; Acts 1:1-11

After Jesus came back to life, He spent many days talking to His friends. One day they went to the top of a hill. "Tell people all over the world about Me," Jesus said. Jesus promised that the Holy Spirit would come and make them able to do everything Jesus asked them to do.

Then Jesus went up to heaven. Jesus' friends watched as Jesus went up in the air. Soon Jesus was covered up by clouds. Jesus' friends couldn't see Him anymore, but they kept looking up for a while.

Suddenly two angels stood beside them. "Why do you stand here
looking into the sky?" They asked. "Jesus will come back someday the same way you saw Him go up into heaven." Then Jesus' friends went to Jerusalem to pray and wait for the Holy Spirit to come.

Jesus goes back to heaven.

Luke 24:50-53; Acts 1:1-11

God sends the Holy Spirit.

Acts 2:1-13

After Jesus went back to heaven, His friends prayed and stayed together in Jerusalem. One morning, a sound like a strong wind blowing filled the house where they were staying. Something that looked like a small fire sat on top of each person's head! The Holy Spirit Jesus promised had finally come!

There were people from many different places staying in Jerusalem. These people spoke many different languages. When they heard the noise, they gathered around the house to see what was going on.

Jesus' friends began to speak in other languages, telling all the people about Jesus. The people in Jerusalem were amazed because they heard what Jesus' friends were saying about Jesus in their own languages! Many people believed in Jesus and started to tell other people about Jesus, too.

God sends the Holy Spirit.

Acts 2:1-13

Jesus talks to Saul.

Acts 9:1-19

Saul was certain that Jesus' friends were telling lies. Saul didn't believe that Jesus was God's Son. Saul wanted to make people stop talking about Jesus. Saul was so angry that he even wanted to kill people who believed in Jesus!

Saul went to Damascus to find people who believed in Jesus and take them as prisoners to Jerusalem. As he walked along the road with some friends, a bright light suddenly flashed around Saul. Saul fell to the ground. Jesus talked to Saul. "Why are you hurting me?" Jesus said. "Go to Damascus and you will be told what you must do." Saul got up, but he could not see. Saul's friends helped Saul walk to Damascus.

For three days, Saul was blind and he didn't eat anything. He prayed to God. God sent a man who loved Jesus to help Saul. The man went to the house where Saul was staying and said, "The Lord Jesus sent me so that you may see again." Right away, Saul could see. Now Saul loved and obeyed Jesus.

Jesus talks to Saul.
Acts 9:1-19

Paul and Silas sing praise to God in jail.

Acts 16:16-40

Paul and his friend Silas were put in jail because some people were angry with them. The jailer put chains on their feet. Paul and Silas didn't act afraid.

Paul and Silas sang songs and prayed to God. The other prisoners in the jail listened to Paul and Silas.

In the middle of the night, the ground began to shake and the walls of the jail began to crumble. There was a terrible earthquake and all the doors of the jail came open. The chains on Paul and Silas came off!

The jailer thought that all the prisoners had escaped. The jailer decided that it would be better to kill himself than to be punished for losing the prisoners.

Paul cried out, "Don't hurt yourself! We are all still here!" The jailer took Paul and Silas out of the jail and took them home to take care of them. Now the jailer wanted to know about Jesus. Everyone in the jailer's family heard the good news about Jesus and believed in Him.

Paul and Silas sing praise to God in jail.
Acts 16:16-40

Paul's ship wrecks in a storm.

Acts 27:1-44

Paul and many other people climbed onto a big ship. Paul knew it would not be safe to travel on the sea at this time. He told the people on the ship, "If we sail now, we'll have problems." The people didn't listen. The wind began to blow. It blew the ship out to sea.

Then the wind began to blow harder and harder. Splash! Splash! The waves splashed high in the air and into the ship. The waves almost knocked the ship over! Big dark clouds covered the sky. The rain came pouring down. Everyone on the ship was afraid. Paul had good news for the people. "Don't be afraid," Paul said. "No one will be hurt. God sent an angel to tell me that God will take care of all of us."

Early in the morning, the people saw land! They tried to sail to the shore. But the big, strong waves pushed the ship into some sand just under the water. Crash! The ship broke apart into little pieces. All the people jumped into the water. They found their way to the land. No one had been hurt. God took care of all the people.

Paul's ship wrecks in a storm.
Acts 27:1-44

Paul writes letters to help others follow Jesus.

2 Timothy 1:1—4:22

Paul wrote many letters to different churches and to different people. Paul wanted to tell others about Jesus. He wanted to help people who loved Jesus know the right things to do. Sometimes Paul wrote letters while he was on a trip. Sometimes he even wrote letters when he was in prison!

Paul wasn't put in prison because he did anything wrong. Paul was put in prison several times because some people didn't want him to tell other people about Jesus.

One time Paul was in a deep, dark dungeon. He wrote a letter to Timothy. Timothy was Paul's friend. Paul wanted to tell Timothy many things. Paul also wanted Timothy to come and visit him in prison. Paul helped Timothy learn how to live as a follower of Jesus.

Paul writes letters to help others follow Jesus.
2 Timothy 1:1—4:22

John writes good news.
Revelation 1:1,2,9-11; 21:3-5

When Jesus lived on earth, John was one of Jesus' best friends. One day Jesus went back to live with God in heaven. Then John told many people the good news that Jesus loves all people. But some people did not love Jesus. They did not like John, either. They took John away from his home and made him live on a lonely island.

John had to stay on the island for a long, long time. Every day he thought about Jesus and prayed. One day when John was praying, something very special happened. John heard a voice say, "Write a book about the things you see. Then send the book to the people who love Me." John knew it was Jesus speaking to him!

Then Jesus showed John what heaven is like. He also showed John some things will happen later. Jesus is going to come back! People who love Jesus will live with Him forever.
For many, many days John carefully wrote Jesus' words on special books called scrolls. In our Bible, we can read the words about heaven that Jesus told John to write.

John writes good news.

Revelation 1:1,2,9-11; 21:3-5

Thank you for your purchase!

Dear valued customer,

We hope your child will enjoy our book!

Please consider leaving a review on Amazon. We would love to hear your feedback as we always trying to create better and better books.

We read every one of your thoughtful messages, and reviews are the best way to let other potential customers know about the book.

We are forever grateful to you!

Want free goodies?
Write the title of your purchase
as the subject of the email
Email us at:
genestudio01@gmail.com

QUESTIONS & CUSTOMER SERVICE?
Email us at:
genestudio01@gmail.com

Rate Me

The cover of this book is made with materials from www.vectezy.com